WORLD'S MOST JACKED ATHLETE

Michael Ray Garvin

ISBN 978-1-68197-245-9 (paperback)
ISBN 978-1-68197-246-6 (digital)

Christian Faith Publishing, Inc.
296 Chestnut Street
Meadville, PA 16335
www.christianfaithpublishing.com

Printed in the United States of America

I would like to acknowledge these
photographers for some great pictures.

Gene Williams

Rivals.com

Scout.com

Cameron Mellor Photography

Mel Evans

FOREWORD

People view athletes today as role models or idols who are above the average society. They have God-given abilities that allow them to perform tasks that a majority of the world cannot do. People also view athletes as being illiterate and drug cheats who made their way to greatness by using illegal drugs. I am writing this book to change the perception of athletes and to show that not all athletes are the same. When a person is looking at a picture of an insanely jacked athlete, I want my book to give that person an option not to jump to a conclusion that he or she is an illegal steroid user, but an athlete who took the natural route.

The picture on the cover of this book has been circulating the Internet since 2009. Many people have seen the picture and automatically assume I took performance-enhancing drugs or illegal steroids. I am here to tear down the stereotypes and assumptions and give truth. In this book, I will share my sports history, training, and supplement regimen so the world can know how I became known as the world's most jacked athlete.

Chapter 1

My Beginning

I was born in Brooklyn, New York, Bedford-Stuyvesant on September 29, 1986. My parents are Johnny Ray Garvin and Adrienne Burgess.

My dad was an athlete. He played high school football and ran track and field. He later received a full scholarship to Adam State College in Pueblo, Colorado. His main position on the football team was defensive back and was a kick returner on special teams. After college, he went to the farm team of the Oakland Raiders and later went to the USFL United States Football League.

My mom was also an athlete. She ran track in high school and later competed in amateur bodybuilding. My two younger brothers Jabari Ray and Jelani Ray, both played football and ran track and field.

I came from a family of athletes, which helped me to excel, but there are many people who have athletic gifts and do not know how to reach their full potential. I will show you how I used knowledge and strategic methods to reach my full potential in sports and training.

When I was three years old, my dad put a football in my hand and taught me how to play football. One day, my dad took me to the track, and I ran four laps without stopping. As a kid, I loved to run and was always energetic.

In the private school I attended, we had a school event, and I was the last leg on the relay race. I was not paying attention when it was my turn to run, and it caused us to fall behind. I ran as fast as I could, caught up to everyone, and we ended up winning the relay race.

Later, we moved from Canarsie in Brooklyn, New York, to Teaneck, New Jersey. I was excited for peewee football because the peewee football teams in New Jersey were a lot better than New York. Many athletes in New York played basketball as their main sport.

My first time playing organized football, I played for the Teaneck Highwaymen. That first year was difficult for me because I never played contact football before, and I did not know the fundamentals of properly hitting or tackling. I was seven years old at this time, and I had to get used to the contact sport. It wasn't until my second year on the team that I got better at the sport. We went undefeated, and I played quarterback. I was the fastest on the team, and every time the coach wanted to score, he would call quarterback sneak. That season I had ten touchdowns and was offensive MVP. One of my good memories was my dad taking me to Wendy's after the game to get a burger and french fries.

I joined a track club called the Englewood Striders and my best races were the four hundred and two hundred meters. My first year running track, I qualified for the AAU National Championships and placed twelfth overall in the two hundred meters.

At the age of ten, my dad purchased a Power Tower gym set where I did push-ups, dips, pull-ups, chin-ups, and knee raises for core work. The first night after we set it up, he taught me the proper technique for pull-ups and chin-ups. He would have me do three sets of ten reps, and my rest in between would be one minute. At first, I was not able to get all ten reps, but with his help every night, I got better. Soon, I was able to get ten reps on pull-ups and chin-ups on my own. I started to notice that my physique was changing. I remember flexing in front of the mirror to see how my chest was developing, and my arms were getting bigger. I also started working out in the basement with my dad where he had a small weight room with dumbbells. I was able to bench press the barbell by itself which weighs 45 lbs. for ten reps. For dumbbell work, I would do three sets of ten reps for dumbbell step-ups and dumbbell lunges. For upper body, I did three sets of ten reps on dumbbell flat bench press and dumbbell incline press.

My stepmom, Tami Powell, would buy milk for me, and I would eat chicken and lunch meat for more protein. I was not big on eating vegetables or fruits at that time. My diet did not become great until I got out of college. I would eat fast food every now and then, but a majority of the time, I had a home-cooked meal. I will go more into detail about my diet later, but for a ten-year-old boy, I was pretty disciplined when it came to working out and sticking to a plan. There were two things that drove me to continue to work hard every night on that power tower gym: one was to get stronger and faster and two was to build my physique. I have to admit, vanity did grow in me at an early age.

I turned my training up a notch, and my dad later signed me up for Parisi School of Speed, which did help me learn the fundamentals of training. My dad and I would wake up at 6:00 a.m. before school, and we would run at the track. My best event was the eight hundred meters, so my workouts were geared toward that race. Those were some of the toughest workouts I've ever had. Even when I wanted to quit, there was a voice always in my head telling me to keep going and to push harder. Sometimes I would cry after those workouts because the pain was intense. As a kid, I wanted to please my father and make him proud of me. Quitting was not an option. After the workouts, I noticed my endurance increasing, and running the races became much easier. That year, I became a state champion while holding the record for my age group. I also earned the title Regional Champion. I did not attend nationals that year for USATF because it was on the West Coast, which was too far from New Jersey. My time at regionals would have given me a shot to become a national champion because it was the second best time in the nation.

Later, I got invited and competed in the Hershey National Championships and placed first in the four hundred meters. After receiving that gold medal and looking back on the season, it finally hit me that hard work actually pays off. What you put in is what you get out. The tears from those brutal morning workouts on the track plus the pain from the lactic acid shooting throughout my whole body was all worth it.

CHAPTER 2

My First Supplements

I was twelve years old when I purchased my first supplement called Stim-O-Stam. I was at the USATF Championships, and there was a booth where they were selling supplements. A representative was telling me about Stim-O-Stam, which helps reduce lactic acid while delaying the onset of fatigue and prevents cramping. The phosphate fuels in the product also help athletes increase their ATP (adenosine triphosphate) levels more quickly once they have been depleted due to exertion. I used the cash that my parents gave me for my trip, and I purchased a bottle to try it out. I was running the four hundred meters, and I took the amount of pills the bottle suggested before my race. During the race, I noticed a difference in my endurance levels. I would usually get tired around the 150-meter mark, but I did not start feeling lactic acid until the eighty-meter mark toward the end of the four hundred meters. I was sold on the product and still take this supplement today. Stim-O-Stam is a supplement you should plan to take throughout your whole life of competition in sports for any athletic event.

I was still competing in the same sports two years later, and I added a second supplement, which was ginseng. The first time I purchased the supplement, I had to chop them up because I was not good at swallowing pills. I remember one of my teammates made fun of me because I looked like a scientist. Science was always my favorite class in school.

Ginseng is an all-natural herb that helps with energy levels. It is an adaptogenic herb, meaning the herb adapts to whatever the body may be lacking. It can counter the effects of stress and enhance intellectual and physical performance. I mainly used the herb for energy and endurance increase.

CHAPTER 3

Don Bosco Freshman

I attended Don Bosco Preparatory High School in 2001. We ran forty-yard dashes on the track, and my time was a 4.57 hand time. I was upset with myself because I wanted to be faster than the seniors Dorien Bryant and Ryan Grant who both went on to play football at Division 1 schools. As a freshman, I played in one varsity game and scored a touchdown. Later on, my dad and I made the decision that I would play freshman and junior varsity football so that I could lift weights and develop into a stronger athlete. During the football season, my good friend Anthony Ferla recommended that I do personal training at a facility owned by Mike Padula. The trainer whom I worked with was Kevin Ensenat. The first night I was there for my assessment test and on the bench press, I maxed out at 225 lbs.

They were shocked because I was a freshman and weighed 164 lbs., but I was benching 225 lbs. Some people may say it was all genetics, but I started doing calisthenics and dumbbell work when I was just ten years old. I already had four years of weight training underneath my belt. Yes, I have good genetics, but I also trained hard and was disciplined.

After talking with both trainers, my dad signed me up, and we started training during my freshman football season. The workouts that Kevin put me through were mainly dumbbell work. He was very knowledgeable on building foundations before trying to build mansions. When you focus on dumbbell work, you are focusing on balancing your body out and strengthening your stabilizing muscles. Many kids and high school coaches immediately try squats or bench press but fail to realize that the majority of the injuries in high school are back issues. Most kids have a weak lower back, core, and hips. They also struggle with improper technique. You should strengthen up the lower back by doing good mornings and deadlifts before you get to squatting. Shoulder problems arise due to incorrect form and technique or not strengthening the anterior and posterior deltoids.

We started off with dumbbell step-ups and dumbbell lunges. We used the split system where one day is a full upper-body workout, and another day is a full lower body. For example:

> Lower-Body Dumbbell (DB) Step-Ups 5x5 reps
> DB Lunges 5x5
> DB Single Leg Split Squat 3x7
> DB Single Stiff Leg Deadlift 3x10
> Calf Raises 3x20
> Abdominals 3x20

The lower body workout would be done within forty-five minutes. Energy levels last about forty-five minutes. If you are lifting for more than an hour, then you are doing too much and may need to consider changing your program. You can lift twice a day, but there needs to be a rest period of at least two hours. You have to know how to supplement properly to help prevent DOMS (delayed onset muscle soreness). If you get into overtraining, it can really hinder your performance in your sport. When I was twelve, it was the first time I experienced overtraining. I got to USATF National Championships. I was tired and had no legs left in me to compete. I ran too many races during the season, and I was burned out. My dad and I both learned a lesson from that experience to monitor your races and training.

For upper body, we would also work with dumbbells to make sure my body was in balance and to strengthen stabilizing muscles. Even though I could bench 225 lbs. as a freshman, there was an imbalance in my arms. Dumbbell training worked great to correct that imbalance. Soon, I was able to bench 100 lb. dumbbells in each hand for a total of ten reps.

CHAPTER 4

Freshman Supplements

The supplements that Kevin recommended me to take was whey protein and BCAAs (branched chain amino acid). The protein drinks that I would drink after each workout was called RTD 51 by Met-Rx. These protein shakes were really good because they had 51 grams of protein. The BCAAs I took was in pill form. I do not remember the exact amount or the ratio of the supplement. I did take more than the recommended dosage. I would sometimes perform extra weight room workouts in my basement and supplement right after to help me recover faster. Another supplement that I added my freshman year was L-arginine-ornithine. This was the Vitamin Shoppe brand that had about 2,000 mg. from each serving. I started taking this supplement to help increase my nitric oxide levels, which help dilate the blood vessels. Nitric oxide helps you have that pump feeling during and after your workout. Arginine is also beneficial to promoting secretion of different hormones like glucagon, insulin, and growth hormone. L-arginine with ornithine has been shown to increase levels of growth promoting hormones. This would have to be taken in high dosages in order to see results. I would normally take eight to ten pills a day in order to help raise my HGH levels at bedtime. Some people ask why I would try to increase my HGH levels at the age of fifteen. Well, there are some people in this world who want to be good or elite. I wanted to be beyond that.

During this time, I was constantly studying on my own about vitamins and minerals. I was learning how they can help benefit me in training. I did not play PlayStation all day. I was in my room, studying how to get every advantage naturally. Most people became great by cheating or using an illegal substance. I wanted to be great naturally. If it took three to four hours of studying about supplements, then I sacrificed my time to get the results.

A big motivator for me while working out and lifting in my basement was watching *Dragon Ball Z*. I absolutely loved this cartoon because the characters were jacked, fast, strong, and powerful. My favorite character was Goku because no matter the situation he was in, he never quit. He always fought hard and somehow found a way to win. He had a tremendous amount of perseverance. Goku and the other fighters would always train at extreme levels to push their bodies to the limit. I wanted to look like Goku and train like him to obtain extreme levels in fitness and become the best all-around athlete.

During track season, I broke the state record for the one hundred meters for the freshman class. My time was 10.98, and the previous time was 10.99 FAT (fully automatic time), which was previously held by the great Carl Lewis. The training and supplements that Kevin recommended helped me become faster and stronger. My supplement regimen was Stim-O-Stam, BCAAs, and RTD 51. My weight did increase, which also helped give me a chance to start on varsity as a sophomore.

CHAPTER 5

Bosco Sophomore

I started at defensive back and wide receiver. Our season was great. I had seven touchdowns and one interception. We also won a state championship. We beat Bergen Catholic for the title. Bergen Catholic was the team Brian Cushing played for and now plays for the Texans. Our player to player rival did not start until our junior year in high school.

I was getting multiple schools interested in me as a player because my speed was eye-catching. I would run past defenders with ease. Marquise Liverpool and I would destroy defensive backfields because of our great route running and speed. Nunzio Campanile was our offensive coordinator, and he had a variety of offensive plays. Mike Teel, our quarterback, threw perfect passes to help us score.

In track and field, I was increasing in speed. It was not my best year because a majority of my training went toward football combines.

I attended the Syracuse University football camp in 2002 and was tested in the forty-yard dash and ran a time of 4.38 and 4.41. At the camp, there was a high school coach who told me that my kind of speed needs to be down south in Florida. His words had an influence on my life because my interests quickly turned to Florida colleges. Running a 4.38 as a sophomore in high school is elite. I had a year of training, and my time went from a 4.57 to a 4.38 in the forty-yard dash.

I added my supplement regimen, and the first supplement was creatine. I was taking creatine monohydrate. This type of creatine had a loading phase to where you had to take higher doses in order for it to absorb into your bloodstream. This creatine also brought stomach discomfort with it. I started taking it toward the end of my sophomore football season. Once in my system, I noticed that my energy levels increased. I also felt more of a nitric oxide pump when working out. Creatine is a naturally occurring micronutrient. It's great for helping to increase fast twitch muscle fiber type 2 A and B. Your muscles, when using fast twitch, use the ATP/CP energy pathway which is adenosine triphosphate/creatine phosphate. Your muscles can feed off this energy pathway without oxygen for ten seconds. Creatine is also good for increasing muscle mass as well. In order for your muscles to operate, they need creatine because it's part of a major energy pathway. You can also get creatine naturally from eating steak. The Greeks would eat steaks before competition to bulk up before they competed in their Olympic events.

There have been a lot of rumors about creatine that are not true. As a high school kid, I am glad that I was on creatine. This supplement helped take my speed, strength, and power to another level. I have been taking creatine since I was fifteen years old, and I have been on it for thirteen years. I have not had any bad experiences with creatine and no harsh side effects at all. It is important to drink water and stay hydrated. Drinking water should already be in your daily regimen if you are an athlete or not. Water helps your body work more efficiently. Some people believe creatine can affect your kidneys. If you are taking creatine in the wrong amounts, it can have an effect. You can help protect your kidneys from harsh chemicals taking a green superfood supplement. I talk more about the green superfood supplement in chapter 18. If you are a parent and have a high school kid around the age of fifteen or older who wants to step up his game to get scholarships, I would suggest allowing them to take creatine.

My trainer switched up my creatine supplement when he ordered Creatine Edge made by FSI Nutrition. This creatine is an effervescent formula where it would balance the Ph levels in your stomach so you can fully absorb the creatine. Another positive with this supplement is that it would not give me stomach discomfort like creatine monohydrate. This Creatine Edge has sodium bicarbonate, which helps retain water and also buffers lactic acid build up. It delays the onset of pyruvic acid turning into lactic acid, which can prevent muscle contraction when training. This creatine allowed me to train harder and longer with less burn. I have been taking this same product since I was sixteen years old. It works, and I never switched up my creatine supplement. FSI Nutrition later became eight-ball nutrition, and I am a sponsored athlete.

The second supplement I added was Horny Goat Weed by GNC. I took this supplement because of the energy boost that I got from it. The GNC brand had a synergistic blend of Horny Goat Weed *(Epimedium sagittatum)* standardized to 10 percent Icariin. Horny Goat Weed is known as an aphrodisiac supplement, which helps naturally boost testosterone levels. It also works as a libido booster. Maca extract, which is an herb from Peru, has multiple vitamins, minerals, amino acids, and plant sterols. It also works to help boost libido and helps increase your energy levels. I've always used this as an alternative to caffeine. Caffeine is a stimulant which borrows energy from the body and does not actually give the body nutrients. Caffeine does make me jittery and nervous, which is not good when playing football. I know caffeine is notorious for causing cramps, dehydration, and muscle pains. The other ingredient in Horny Goat Weed was Mucuna pruriens extract. It was standardized to 15 percent L-Dopa. L-Dopa is a precursor to dopamine, which is a neurotransmitter that helps control mood, cognitive function, and motor control. The last ingredient was Polypodium vulgare extract, which had the root and the rhizome. They are similar to ecdysteroids, plant and insect hormones or another name steroids. They get the name from ecdysis, which is a process insects use to break from their shells or change in form. These ecdysteroids do not affect male or female hormones at all. They connect to a receptor in the human body, which uses this for protein synthesis. In other words, they only benefit to build muscle.

Supplement List:

Creatine Edge
L-arginine-ornithine
BCAAs
RTD51
Horny Goat Weed
Stim-O-Stam

Training with Kevin advanced to a lot of deadlifting in the off-season. I remember we would deadlift with chains and off a six-inch box. My shins would always get scraped from deadlifting because it's important to keep the bar as close as possible to maintain form. My best deadlift was when I did 500 lbs. on the box. It is a lot harder than normal deadlifting because you have to reach lower to lift the bar. There were plenty of days that I hated doing deadlifts because they were difficult, but I always showed up ready to work. I was sometimes impatient and wanted to squat because everyone else was squatting, but I listened to my trainer and trusted the program. Some athletes don't see benefits because they either do not trust the program or feel like they know more than their trainer.

CHAPTER 6

Bosco Junior

I started at wide receiver, defensive back, and played some running back. The first day that I was able to receive a scholarship, I got one in the mail from Rutgers University. The head coach at the time was Greg Schiano. He was a great coach, and Rutgers is a great school. I always wanted to go down south where it was warm. I also believed that the best players were down south, and I always wanted to compete against the best. The majority of the athletes we ran against in track and field who were elite were either from California, Texas, or Florida. I also had other scholarship offers from different schools like Boston College and Syracuse. After my junior football season, more scholarships came in.

I rushed for 615 yards on seventeen carries and I scored six touchdowns. As a defensive back, I had four interceptions and took two of them back for touchdowns. I had a total of eight touchdowns my junior year. I was all-metro, all-state, all-county, and all-league at defensive back in New Jersey.

Track season, I progressed and ran times of 10.6 in the one hundred meters. My two hundred-meter time was 21.7, and I would split fifty-one in the 4x400 meter relay. I always hated running the 4x4 relay especially after running the one hundred and two hundred meters. Sometimes I had to compromise with my track coach to get out of the race. That year, I became a track and field All-American in the one hundred meters and two hundred meters when I competed in the Nike Outdoor National Championships.

In January of 2004, I attended the U.S Army Combine in San Antonio, Texas. My forty-yard dash time was a 4.37 and 4.41. The 4.37 solidified me as the fastest man at the combine, and I was named the defensive MVP of the combine. I locked down many wide receivers at defensive back.

I started to receive more scholarship offers after the U.S Army Combine, and I had about ten scholarship offers. I later attended a Nike Camp to get more attention from schools. My dad and I agreed on going to the Nike camp in Palo Alto at Stanford University. I also went with my friend Anthony Ferla who played high school football at Saint Joes. I was extremely confident in my speed, strength, and talents. Mentally, I was one of the best cornerbacks in the nation, and I wanted to prove that. After my performance at the US Army combine, I wanted to dominate even more. I ran a 4.28 in the forty-yard dash in front of the college scouts. This was on wet grass because it had rained the night before. I also bench pressed 185 lbs. for twenty-four reps. They had the offensive lineman bench press 225 lbs. and skill players bench 185 lbs. because we were only in high school. My weight was 175 lbs. and my height was 5'8". I ran my short shuttle in 4.41, which is not good, but it was hard to get a grip because of the wet grass. My vertical jump was a 32.8 inches, which was okay, but I needed to improve it especially for a defensive back at my height.

In the one-on-one drills, I was very confident and decided to do press coverage. I covered Desean Jackson, and he tried to go deep on the first route. I was right there on his hip, and he did not catch the ball. Throughout the whole one-on-one drill, I only had one pass caught on me, and I covered about seven athletes. I also left that camp as the fastest man, and it felt good. I knew I was fast, but now the rest of America was starting to find out that I was a legit speedster.

The last combine that I attended my junior year was the Elite College Combine. I remember getting into a small dispute with my dad because I did not want to go. I felt like I had already made a name for myself and did not need to do any more testing. He was right for bringing me to this combine because I became a nationally recruited athlete. We went to Rutherford New Jersey to the New York Giants Practice facility. There were a lot of big-time athletes there who went to the National Football League like me. The big name athletes who attended were Derrick Williams (Detroit Lions), Brian Cushing (Houston Texans), LeSean McCoy (Buffalo Bills), Eugene Monroe (Jacksonville Jaguars), and Myron Rolle (my teammate at Florida State and former NFL player).

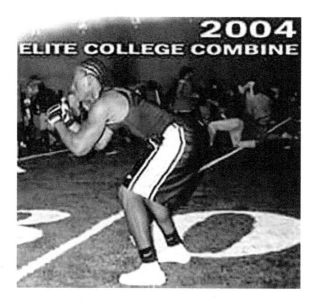

Everyone there was saying that Derrick Williams was the fastest man, and we haven't even ran the forty-yard dash yet. Derrick walked in with his USA track and field gear, but that did not faze me. I was just eager to run the forty, so I could show these college scouts my speed. There were a bunch of scouts from the Big East, Big Ten, ACC, and some SEC schools. I don't remember seeing any Big 12 schools.

After they took our height and weight, they warmed us up for the forty-yard dash. My first forty, I had a quick start and ran a time of 4.18. The Notre Dame scout told me that I had to run it again and to hold a little longer on my start. On my second attempt, I held longer for a second and took off. I posted a time of 4.22, and the scouts still didn't believe it. I ran it a third time and posted a time of 4.28, and they said that my time was too fast for a high school athlete. After we did all our position drills to warm up for one-on-ones, they asked me to run the forty-yard dash one more time. I posted a time of 4.30. They made that my official time, and it was the fastest time of the combine. The second best time was from the athlete Derrick Williams whom they thought was the fastest man in the building, but after testing, results showed otherwise.

Now I had to prepare for one-on-one drill and show my cover skills. My heart started to beat a little faster, and adrenaline was flowing because this was a huge event. Once the first play is out of the way, you become more relaxed and into the zone. As an athlete, you forget that people are there watching. When you are in the zone, it's just you and the opponent. I purposely chose to cover Derrick Williams because I wanted to show these scouts that I was fast and could cover the best receiver in the building. I think I covered about eight times, and I only had two balls caught on me. Nyan Boateng caught a fade route, and another receiver caught a short out route. The rest of the routes that Derrick Williams ran, I locked him down, and I had three pass break-ups on him.

After the combine was over, I had multiple coaches come up to me and told me I did a great job. University of Georgia scout was very interested in me, and a couple days later, I had more scholarships pouring in. The Florida State scout was at the Elite College Combine, saw me compete, and offered me a scholarship. I also had scholarships to Notre Dame, University of Miami, Penn State,

University of Michigan, University of Georgia, and the University of Florida. I had a total of fifty-five scholarships. I had a box full of letters from colleges, and I was truly thankful and grateful. Many athletes would give anything to have just one scholarship from a division one school, and God blessed me with fifty-five. I never took it for granted. When you are a highly recruited player and nationally known with big time scholarships, pride starts to sneak in, and it is very important to stay humble.

The training that Kevin put me through was progressing. We finally got into squatting. We did regular squats, four-second negative squats, box squats, and Romanian rhythm squats. The Romanian rhythm squats were my favorite because I did those four days before my track meet, and I had a personal best in the one hundred meters. For upper body, I was maxing out at 305 lbs. on bench press. I was also able to do pull-ups with a 120-lb. dumbbell strapped to my waist for multiple reps. I did dips with a 120-lb. dumbbell strapped to my waist for about three reps. Kevin helped turn me into a machine. During my workouts, whenever we would go up in weight I would tell myself, "Don't fear the weight. Let the weight fear you." We also had a slight competition against Brian Cushing and Joe Defranco. Brian Cushing was Bergen Catholic's best athlete, and I was Don Bosco Prep's best athlete. Whenever we played against each other, it was always a good game. Joe Defranco would train mainly the Bergen Catholic athletes, and Kevin Ensenat would train a lot of the Don Bosco athletes. It was always a friendly rivalry with mutual respect as players. We never talked trash to each other. We always had a friendly competition.

My supplement regimen was still the same. I did add a joint support supplement that had white willow bark, turmeric, and shark cartilage in it. It also contained glucosamine and MSM.

CHAPTER 7

Bosco Senior

This was my best year for football and track and field. I started at running back and defensive back. I rushed for 1,600 yards and scored thirty-four touchdowns. I also had fifty tackles as a defensive back and recorded three interceptions. We finished the season at 10–2. We lost the state championship game, which was tough. We won the state championship my junior year and was ranked the number 2 team in the nation. Bergen Catholic finally beat us, and Brian Cushing had a great game. After the state championship game, I was going to commit to Florida State University. I remember the day after I committed to FSU, Urban Meyer called my dad and wanted me to come to Florida University and play for him. Urban Meyer was recruiting heavily, especially players with tremendous speed. I told him I'm going to FSU to become a Seminole. I wanted to play at FSU because of the dynasty. They had Deion Sanders, Peter Warrick, Warrick Dunn, and all the other great athletes. They also had a lot of speed, and I wanted to keep the tradition going. I told myself that if I can play at FSU, I can play in the league because all of the great players came from the Florida Schools. Miami, Florida, and FSU were still top teams in the nation when I was recruited.

I was now preparing for the 2005 U.S. Army All-American Game held in San Antonio. To prepare, I put my pads on a week before so I could get used to hitting and moving in pads. The week of the U.S. Army game, we got treated like celebrities. We had multiple interviews, and we had great competition amongst ourselves. I remember Justin King and I raced each other, and I beat him. When two fast athletes meet each other, there is going to be a race because of competitiveness. I was good enough to play both ways in the game so I ran routes as a receiver. During practice, I had to cover Fred Rouse a couple times who was the number 1 receiver in the nation, and he was going to Florida State. We had some really good battles out there. It was a fun week building camaraderie with other great players, who were also one day going to the National Football League.

In track, I broke many records in the one hundred meters and two hundred meters. I skipped my senior prom because I had a track meet the next day. I stayed home and lifted weights and watched *Dragon Ball Z*. Most people will laugh, but the next day, I broke the one-hundred-meter record and the two-hundred-meter record. Some of the other athletes on my team did not compete as well because they drank alcohol. I didn't care about prom; my focus was on becoming a great athlete and making it to the NFL. I became a state champion in the one hundred meters running a time of 10.50, and I placed second in the two hundred meters running a time of 21.31. I later went on to the 2005 Nike Outdoor National Championships and placed third in the one hundred meters, recording a time of 10.46, which was my personal best. I raced against J-Mee Samuels who went to Arkansas and Jacoby Ford who placed fifth. Jacoby Ford later went to Clemson University and to the Oakland Raiders. I got fifth place in the two hundred meters running a time of 21.43.

It felt great to be a two-sport All-American in football and track and field. Not many athletes get the accolades of becoming an All-American in one sport, and I am truly grateful and thankful.

I always trained during the football season with Kevin because I wanted to maintain the gains that I had from summer workouts. Many high school athletes go throughout the whole football season and stop lifting weights. They have no clue that it can affect your game. The lifting during the season was not as heavy as off-season lifting. It was more of a maintenance workout. There were times where I would go a little heavy earlier during the week or if I had a bye week. Whenever I lifted and played in the game on Friday night, I felt really strong. I felt faster and stronger because I did not lose muscle during the season. After the football season, we got back into squatting, and we went pretty heavy. We did rack squats, and I would do 405 lbs. for two reps and 365 lbs. for six reps. We also used chains and hooks. The hooks would hook to the outside of the barbell, and there was weight attached to the hooks. On the negative of the squat, once I reached parallel, the hooks would pop off, and the weight would become lighter. I would focus on exploding up on the positive concentric movement. This would help trigger fast twitch muscle fiber type 2 A and B. We also used a yolk, which is good for balance and proprioception work or, in another term, body awareness. Kevin later went overseas for a week to learn some crucial workouts to try on me to help take me to that next level. A good way to know if a program works is trial and error. There are a lot of programs out there for weight training. Some programs work, and some do not. My workouts were more advanced to where I did not have a whole lot of reps. I did not need it because of the level of training I was at. Some people may need higher reps to begin with. You also have some people doing higher reps to work on the dynamic part of their training, which is also known as speed strength. My barbell flat bench press max was 335 lbs., and I weighed 178 lbs. I have always done a lot of external rotations with dumbbells to help strengthen up my anterior and posterior deltoids. Kevin had me doing this since my freshman year. These exercises helped prevent me from having shoulder injuries. We also did dumbbell frontal, lateral, and bent-over lateral raises, which also worked scapula. My upper-body strength increased, which we expected it to with me growing plus the training and proper supplementation.

We always incorporated single leg work to help prevent knee injuries. Dumbbell single leg split squats helped strengthen my vastus medialis and work glutes.

I've always taken my supplements during any competition. When I realized how much of a benefit they were to my training and results, this was something I knew I had to stay on for the rest of my career. Many people may think legal supplements are not natural, but it's all about perception. I see supplements that are legal as being natural because I have a complete understanding of them. For example, when you eat chicken, it contains the macronutrient protein. Protein in the stomach breaks down into amino acids with the help of the protease enzyme. Instead of eating food and causing your body to waste energy on breaking down the food for energy, it's easier to take the amino acid, which is already broken down into pure energy to save the fuel of your body. In chapter 15, I will share my thought process on optimizing energy levels and why I was so successful at competing and testing in combines.

CHAPTER 8

Seminole Freshman

When I first entered summer training, the defensive backs Trevor Ford, Tony Carter, and JR Bryant gave me the nickname Statue. They thought my physique was built like a statue. Not many college athletes can come in and play their freshman year. I had to step up because Antonio Cromartie injured his knee during summer training. He was the best cornerback on the team. He was athletic but also worked very hard. There is a pressure that surrounds you in football, which comes from your family, coaches, friends, and fans. They have expectations of you, and we being athletes try our best to live up to those expectations. During the summer training, I started hanging out with the wrong crowd and got into smoking marijuana. I had previously tried it before my senior year in high school, but I became a heavier user once I got to college. I used it because it was relaxing, and it helped me forget about the pressure. I do not recommend anyone to smoke marijuana. I have been sober from it since 2009. I'm being transparent to help lead someone in the right direction to learn from my mistakes. The side effects that I did get from marijuana was trouble with short-term memory. My long-term memory was fine. It sometimes took me a little longer to process my thinking, which was a hindrance to me on the football field.

After training camp, I was third string defensive back. Our first game was against Miami in Doak Campbell Stadium. I was so hyped coming out of the tunnel and seeing over eighty thousand people in the stands. It was almost surreal, like a scene from gladiator, but bigger. I didn't get to play in the game, but the entire experience was amazing. I played in the rest of the games that season and moved up from third string to second string.

One of my biggest games was in the ACC Championship game against Virginia Tech. We beat them and ended up going to the Orange Bowl in Miami, Florida. We played against Penn State. It was a big game because two legendary coaches were playing against each other: Bobby Bowden, who was my coach and Joe Paterno, who was head coach of Penn State. Bobby Bowden was the best football coach I ever had. We lost to Penn State in the game in three overtimes. They beat us by a field goal.

That year, I learned a lot and loved playing with Ernie Sims, Broderick Bunkley, Pat Watkins, Willie Reid, Kamerion Wimbley, and Leon Washington. Ernie Sims had a big impact on me. He played linebacker, and he ran about a 4.3 high in the forty yards. Ernie had dog in him. What I mean by dog is he had an attitude about his game that he was going to hit hard and play fast. After seeing Ernie hit a pile of players, and moving that pile, I said to myself, "I want to play just like that." He played with no concern for the well-being of his body when he tackled an athlete. An athlete who plays like that has no fear on the field.

After the season, I was healing from a broken hand that I suffered in the FedEx Orange bowl. I broke my fifth metacarpal in my left hand, and while I was healing, I took calcium supplements to help me heal faster. I was also taking a wheatgrass supplement from Amazing Grass Company. My stepmom told me about this product, and she was taking it herself. Wheatgrass is really good for cleansing and detoxifying the body. The average human being has over seven hundred toxins in their body. Wheatgrass also helps the body balance pH, which is important for preventing cancer. Wheatgrass also contains chlorophyll, which helps increase blood oxygen levels. I could definitely notice a slight energy increase, and it would make bowel movements more frequent.

Training for track season was fun. I was still healing up from my broken hand, and I did not qualify for nationals in indoor track. When outdoor came, I finished with a good season. My one-hundred-meter time was the same 10.46, but my two-hundred-meter time dropped from a 21.31 to a 20.75. I qualified for the finals in the NCAA Outdoor championships. In the two hundred meters, I finished in eighth place, with a time of 21.05. I became an All-American as a true freshman at Florida State.

My supplement regimen changed, and I added a product called Amino Vital Fast Charge. It was an amino acid supplement that would quickly recharge your body. It's one of the best supplements to take before any competition. It has glutamine, arginine, and BCAAs in it. The delivery method was genius because it would replenish your body quickly during an event. I would take the packets before and after my races. I would only take it after a race if I had more than one race that day. I would also do the same with Horny Goat Weed Complex. Sometimes, I would take up to twelve pills a day during a competition. The recommended dose was four pills, and I never experienced any bad side effects. Usually, the recommended dose is for the average human being. I learned that with most supplements I could take more than recommended. It could also mean that I had a hypermetabolism. This means, I metabolize supplements quickly, and I would need more than the recommended dose to see a benefit. I later switched to the Vitamin Shoppe brand of Horny Goat Weed because GNC changed up their formula.

CHAPTER 9

Seminole Junior

I learned a lot as a junior because after my football games, I would go out to drink, smoke marijuana, and I noticed that my level of play was being affected. My body was sore after the game, and drinking alcohol prevented it from recovering at the normal rate. I was starting at defensive back but later was put on the second string. One reason I made a decision to give up alcohol was because it was affecting my game. I noticed that my strength and speed started to increase after completely giving it up. Later on, toward the end of the season, I got my starting job back at defensive back.

I added three supplements to my regimen during my junior year. The first supplement I added was Oxydrene made by Novex Biotech. The formula that they have now is not the original formula. The original formula contained only three herbs. Two of the herbs were grown in the high mountains of Asia. One of the ingredients was Schizandra ginseng, which is an adaptogenic herb. It's good for increasing energy levels. This supplement helped increase my VO2 max naturally. I wanted to be able to train harder and last longer on the football field. I remember researching on the computer for three hours on how to naturally increase my oxygen levels. The reason why this supplement was legal because I was using herbs that were not on the banned substance list of the NCAA.

The other supplement I added was Isa-Test by Isatori labs. Kevin recommended this to me, and at first, I was a little hesitant on taking it. After doing extensive research on the product, I decided to take it. The ingredients in this product are all natural herbs, and there are no prohormones in the supplement. It contains zinc and magnesium, which help increase your own testosterone levels. It has tribulus extract where it's standardized to 60 percent saponins and 20 percent protodioscin. If your test booster has tribulus and not protodioscin in it, then it may not be as effective. You need the saponins and the standardized protodioscin. It also contains Horny Goat Weed, which I mentioned in the previous chapters. Another ingredient is citrus orange peel, which has Hesperidin. It is a bioflavonoid. It is used as a natural estrogen inhibitor. Men and women have both testosterone and estrogen in their body. Testosterone is the male hormone for male characteristics. The more testosterone in a man can cause toned muscles, increased fat burn, and increased strength. Estrogen is the female hormone that men want less of. Isa-Test also contains Fenugreek extract, which is standardized to 50 percent saponins. Fenugreek works by acting like testosterone and attaching itself to testosterone receptors. It helps your own body create more natural testosterone. The ingredient longjack *(Eurycoma longifolia)* is extracted to a 20:1 ratio. This is one of my favorite herbs because it's one of strongest for natural test boosting. It works by triggering the LH or luteinizing hormone, which tells the testicles to produce more testosterone. This herb also works as a natural anti-estrogen and helps lower cortisol levels by almost 30 percent. Isa-test also contains two plants Ajuga turkestanica extract 10:1 and Rhaponticum carthamoides extract standardized for 5 percent ecdysterones. I talked about ecdysteroids before because they were in the Horny Goat Weed Complex. The natural sources of these ecdysteroids are spinach, asparagus, quinoa, yams, and also white button mushrooms. Naturally, we as humans eat these steroids on a daily basis but do not get enough in our diet for it to be beneficial. When you look at the definition of steroids, it breaks down to hormones, plant sterols, and cholesterol. Yes, cholesterol is a steroid. When people are talking about steroids, always makes sure you ask which kind of steroid because there are some that are illegal. The illegal ones are synthetic human and animal hormones. The legal steroids are plant and insect hormones that come from our food. Some people believe they can just eat the plants by themselves to get what they need instead of taking them in a supplement. It's important to understand that the benefits only come from the extracted plant compounds or chemicals. You would have to eat a ton of the herbs just to get a benefit. You would either be full or sick from eating too much. There are many different ways to extract from herbs. You can use alcohol, percolation method, infusion, and decoction.

The herbs in Isa-Test also do not affect or stop your own production of testosterone because it is not a synthetic hormone being placed into the body. When you take synthetic testosterone, the body will recognize it as being testosterone and will not produce its own because it senses there is already enough. Your own body has a regulator that helps it from overloading the body with too much hormones. The human body works synergistically so we as humans can survive.

Some people have tried taking natural test boosters and have not had any success with it. The product that you took probably did not have a good combination of herbs or you did not take enough. The recommended dose for Isa-Test was four pills. I sometimes took twelve pills a day of Isa-Test. I did not experience any side effects.

The third supplement I added was Beta-alanine. Kevin also recommended this supplement for me. Beta-alanine is an amino acid, and it is a precursor for carnosine. Carnosine helps buffer lactic acid. If you can delay lactic acid buildup, you can train longer and harder. It also helps build anaerobic and aerobic endurance. Beta-alanine also helps boost the effects of creatine. Those two supplements are taken together to help your fast twitch muscle fibers work harder and longer. The only thing I did not like about beta-alanine was that it made me itch and sometimes gives a tingling sensation. I experienced the itchy and tingling feeling because it triggers the histamine in the body. When you eat carbohydrates while taking this supplement, it intensifies the effect.

I had some really good results from adding those three supplements to my regimen. My time in the sixty meters dropped from a 6.66 to a 6.63. When I first took beta-alanine, I ran a personal best of 20.90 in the two hundred meters. It was on an indoor bank track at Arkansas. Competing at the NCAA Indoor Championships, I beat my personal best time and ran a 20.75 in the two hundred meters. I was an indoor All-American in the sixty meters and two hundred meters in 2007.

My outdoor season, I was working to improve my one-hundred-meter and two-hundred-meter times from last year. In the one hundred meters, I ran a 10.10, and in the two hundred meters, I ran a 20.58. I got close to those times but did not beat them. I think what hindered me was I started running 4x400 meter relays. I also decided to run an open four hundred meters to see what time I would get. I ran a personal best of 46.61 with no training for the race. I had a pretty good mixture of type 1 and type 2 muscle fiber.

My training by Coach Ken Harnden was also very helpful. I was a well-rounded athlete in the one hundred, two hundred, and four hundred meters. Most sprinters just run the one hundred and two hundred meters because they don't have the endurance for the four hundred meters.

I ran in the Olympic Trials that year for the two hundred meters, and I qualified all the way to the semi-final rounds. I remember Walter Dix, my teammate, destroying the trials by qualifying for the Olympics in the one hundred and two hundred. I always looked up to Walt and tried to mimic his style of running when I was in college. He was a phenomenal sprinter.

CHAPTER 10

Seminole Senior

My last year at FSU, I led the nation in kickoff returns average. My average at one point was 34.1 yards. I finished the season at 30.1 avg. I became an All-American in football and was First-Team All-American by Sporting News and Third Team All-American by *Sports Illustrated*. A lot of that had to do with the coaching of Jody Allen and the blocking of my teammates. If my teammates did not do their job and block for me, it would have been a lot harder. I decided to buy a cake for my teammates that said, "We are All-Americans." I truly believed that it was a team effort that helped me succeed in kickoff returns. It was also a great feeling because I was now a two-sport All-American in high school and college. Not many athletes can say they are Two Sport All-Americans in high school and college. I was also able to break three records at Florida State for kick returns. Two of them are now held by Levonte Whitfield. I am truly grateful and thankful to have those accolades.

After the season, I went back home to New Jersey to train with Kevin for the NFL Draft in 2009. My first day back, Kevin tested me, and I ran a time of 4.39 and 4.43 in the forty-yard dash. I was a little upset because I felt that I should be faster. It was after the football season, and my training at FSU was not the same as with my trainer. As a university strength and conditioning coach, you have limited amount of time with the athletes, so the workouts can't be as advanced, especially when you have over eighty guys to train.

CHAPTER 11

Pro Day Training

I knew the training with Kevin would help me reach my best times. We were doing speed squats, four-second negative squats, barbell split jump squats, and Romanian rhythm squats. We also did plyometric work like box jumps, resistance bands on the barbell, and other explosive training exercises. For upper body, we would lift to build strength. Later on, closer toward pro day, we worked on endurance. The endurance was for the bench press test of 225 lbs. My goal was to get around seventeen to twenty reps. When we first started, I was only able to get thirteen reps.

After each workout, I would work on starts and block starts for track and field. I was going to run my senior year of track while training for my FSU pro day. Running track helped me out tremendously. I was running the sixty meters, and I ran a top 10 time in the world of 6.59. This was at the ACC championship where I took second place behind Jacoby Ford. Most football players fail to understand how to train for the forty-yard dash, which is the most important test of the combine or pro day. The forty-yard dash is thirty-six meters, and I was training for sixty meters running superb times. Many football players only run about thirty yards or forty yards when training for the forty. You have to train your body to run a farther distance than your race. I see many athletes struggling to finish the forty yards because of undertraining. There are some critics who say that track and field is not beneficial towards football players. The majority of the time, it's people who have never ran track or competed in the sport and was not good enough. Being a football player running track benefited me tremendously. I knew how to control and monitor my speed on the football field. I was very good at accelerating and decelerating. As an athlete, you should incorporate this into your training.

There are some players who drop in the draft because their forty-yard time was bad. NFL scouts and teams will not even look at a player if his forty-yard time is not good enough. The NFL puts so much weight on the forty-yard dash. I have seen consensus All-Americans drop in draft stock because their forty-yard time was not ideal.

I competed in the NCAA Indoor championships in 2009 and placed seventh. I became a seven-time All-American in track and field. My pro day was scheduled two days after my race. The race on Friday helped prepare me for pro day on Monday.

CHAPTER 12

FSU Pro day 2009

I weighed in at 174 lbs., and 5'7¾" was my height measurements. I broad jumped a 10'8" and jumped 39" on my first vertical jump. I was told to redo my vertical because my foot slightly moved before I jumped. The NFL Scouts are strict when it comes to testing. After jumping a total of four times, I got a thirty-six-inch vertical. I then did bench press test of 225 lbs., and I got a total of eighteen reps. That was a really good number considering I only weighed 174 lbs. We went to the field to run forty-yard dashes right after the bench press. They give you about fifteen to twenty minutes to rest. I ran a time of 4.18, and on my second attempt, I ran 4.22. On my first run, the scouts asked me to hold a little longer on my start. I held for a longer time and still ran a superb time. These times were hand timed, and they added on time for human error. My official times were 4.24 and 4.28. If you want to time these yourself, you can visit YouTube and type in "Michael Ray Garvin FSU Seminole 2009 NFL Pro Day." You can witness for yourself what a legit 4.1 and 4.2 forty-yard dash looks like.

Chapter 13

Mechanics of the 40

To break down the forty-yard dash, I need to put it in phases for you. There are four phases to the forty-yard dash. You have the start, drive, transition, and top end speed. The start is the key of the race. Your form and technique play a huge role in being explosive and not wasting time. You want to focus on jumping the gun when you start. What I mean by that is, whenever there is a hand time or partial electronic laser, you have a human starting the clock. They have to react off of you in order for the clock to start. You want to focus on staying perfectly still and shooting everything out forward when you decide to take off. The majority of the time scouts will look at the movement of the arm that is up because the start is in a three-point stance (two feet and one hand on the ground). The athlete does not want to have a rolling start because the clock or stopwatch will start early, and it will affect your time. Your first step is also important on the start. I usually get between three feet and four feet on my first step. That is a little over a yard because three feet equals one yard. I tell people I don't run a forty yards. I say I run 38¾ yards because of my initial step.

The drive phase is to about fifteen yds. Your head must stay low, and you want to take huge steps without compromising your dorsiflexion in your feet. In the drive phase, you want a low heel recovery, which helps your feet hit the ground faster. The higher you lift your feet in the drive phase, the longer the distance it is from the ground to propel your forward. I usually get about 6 to 6¼ steps in ten yards. If you can get that, then you should be around a 1.4. It also depends on how explosive you are. You can have power, but you need explosive speed as well. That comes with plyometric training.

The transition phase is fifteen to twenty yards. You slowly raise your head up and transition into a top end speed. This is also where I usually exhale and breathe back in quickly, so I can continue to have fast muscle contraction. You do not want to pop up too fast because you don't want to slow down your momentum. You should keep a slight forward body lean when getting into top end speed.

At top end speed, you are at full speed, and you need to exercise proper running form. High knee drives with dorsiflexion of the feet and snapping the heels toward the butt. Your arms should also be in a ninety-degree angle. The faster your arms move, the faster your legs will move because the body works in sync.

Secret Phase

The last phase of the forty-yard dash that I normally do not mention to people is the overdrive phase. I designed this phase myself. This phase is done within the last five to ten yards of the forty-yard dash. The reason I call it the overdrive phase because my running technique changes to where I am overstriding to gain about 2¾ yards each step. I know it's wrong to run like this because you can pull a hamstring, but I am well advanced enough to be able to handle this phase. I know how to train my hamstrings and make sure my glutes are firing properly. If an athlete really wants to get a faster time he can consider using this phase. An athlete's quad to hamstring ratio should be checked before training to make sure his hamstring is, at least, half the strength of his quad. If your hamstring is less than half, then you need to consider doing fast concentric and slow heavy eccentric lifts. This is to strengthen that muscle and reduce hamstring injuries. The exercises you can do are lying leg curl machine, dumbbell single stiff leg deadlift, and glute-ham raises. I like to compare this phase to redlining in a car. If you redline a car, you have the possibility to damage the transmission. In this phase, you have the possibility to pull a hamstring, but if you don't, your time can be faster. I use this phase during every forty-yard dash that I run. I operate with no fear, and this mentality is what allows me to go farther than the next man. Fear stops a lot of people from being great. It's also important to remember, when you operate in a no-fear mentality, there must also be a balance. Ultimately, you as a person or an athlete have a choice in every situation. If you want to see this phase on video, watch my FSU pro day on YouTube to see me hit this phase in the last ten yds.

Decreasing my time from a 4.39 to a 4.18 and 4.22 is great gains. I want to share with the world my supplementation regimen that helped me perform at a high level.

CHAPTER 14

Pro Day Supplements

I added three more supplements to my regimen. They were Waxy Maize by IDS, Power Drive, and GPLC (Glycine propionyl-L-carnitine).

Waxy Maize is an amylopectin or a gum-base plant. It is a starch, which is a carbohydrate. This carbohydrate's molecular weight is heavier than the normal carbs, like maltodextrin and dextrose. It does not get digested in the stomach. It passes right through to the small intestine where it remains as a long chain carbohydrate for a sufficient amount of energy. This supplement also makes you feel full, so you won't have to eat any food. It floods your muscles with glycogen storage for increased energy. The supplement also helps increase blood volume. The blood volume causes vascularity, which can cause the appearance of a leaner physique. This is one reason why I was very toned in the picture running my forty-yard dash.

GPLC is a supplement that works as a nitric oxide booster, anti-oxidant, and ergogenic aid (physical performance or recovery). This supplement was vital to me after bench pressing 225 lbs. for eighteen reps. I was tired and light-headed. I needed to recover quickly in a short amount of time. After I benched pressed 225 lbs., I took my amino vital fast charge packets, beta-alanine, Horny Goat Weed, Isa-Test, and GPLC chewable to recover for my forty. I would always go to the bathroom to take my supplements because most people who don't have the knowledge will automatically assume you are taking something illegal to boost your performance. Everything I took was legal, but perception means almost everything to a lot of people. I took a majority of my supplements away from the public eye to avoid critics or jealous people stating I'm doing something illegal.

The third supplement was Power Drive by Bio-Test. This supplement was mainly a nootropic. It was energy for the brain. The main ingredient was L-tyrosine, which is a precursor to the neurotransmitters epinephrine, norepinephrine, and dopamine. It also has phosphatidyl-choline and DMAE, which are vital brain nutrients and precursors to the neurotransmitter acetylcholine. This supplement helped me focus, gave me more energy, and helps increase motor control. There have been clinical studies showing this supplement can help you get three extra reps on bench press.

The supplements I took the night before pro day were L-arginine-ornithine and Isa-Test. This helped boost my own HGH levels and testosterone levels. The supplements did not take my testosterone to epitestosterone ratio past 7:1, which was the legal amount for NCAA, WADA, and IOC. In the morning of my pro day, I would mix Creatine Edge with two scoops of Waxy Maize. I also added one scoop of wheatgrass and one scoop of Power Drive. I made an extra drink with everything, except the creatine to take after my forty-yard dash. This helped keep my body refueled throughout the day.

My thought process is to energize before and after each test, which exerted a lot of my energy. Let me give you an analogy. If you want to drive from New York to Florida, you have to have enough gas to reach your destination. On the way, it's important to make stops to refuel your car. If you want to perform at a certain level, you have to make sure your body has the energy to reach that level. A CLS 550 Mercedes-Benz is more powerful than a Honda Civic. The Mercedes-Benz takes premium gas, and the Honda Civic takes regular gas. You cannot put regular gas into the Mercedes-Benz. It will not run at optimal performance. If you are an athlete, then you need premium fuel. I always looked at energy like the three levels of gasoline. For specific cars, you have 87, 89, and 93 gas. Regular food from the grocery store is 87 gas and organic food is 89 gas. Supplements are 93 gas because they help a high-performance athlete run at his most optimal level. I also used a simple principle that is normally used in training, but for supplements. The principle is the SAID principle which is specific adaptive imposed demand. I used specific supplements to manipulate my body to do what I wanted. It's easy to do things the illegal the way, but it's always better to have integrity so you can sleep at night. A majority of NFL pro days have no drug testing being done by the schools. I want to mention that I was specifically drug tested days later by the Indianapolis Colts, and I took a blood test for them. There were no issues with my test because I was clean.

CHAPTER 15

Professional Career

I was the fastest man in the 2009 NFL Draft. I was signed to the Arizona Cardinals as an undrafted free agent. The cardinals wanted to switch me to wide receiver because of my speed. They wanted to use me like Devin Hester when he was the return man for the Chicago Bears. I had to quickly learn the offense and how to play wide receiver again. It was truly a blessing to learn from Anquan Boldin and Larry Fitzgerald. Anquan took me under his wing because we both were FSU alumni. I made a lot of plays and was working my way up for the coaches to see me as a valuable player. My head coach was Ken

Whisenhunt, and my wide receiver coach was John Mcnulty. My first NFL training camp was fun, and I was eager to compete for a spot on the team. Getting cut was never a thought in my head. There were many times that I showed my speed, and people were amazed. I was able to move fluidly and make cuts without slowing down a lot. In the first NFL Preseason game, we played against the Pittsburgh Steelers. This game was like a rematch because the cardinals lost to them earlier that year in the Super Bowl. I got in the game in the third quarter, and on my first kick return, I almost froze up. After getting that return, I felt comfortable and was in the zone. I averaged thirty yards on four kick returns and ten yards on three punt returns. I also had one catch for twelve yards. I had 172 all-purpose yards and an Arizona reporter gave me MVP of the game. During the game, I got hurt, and my knee was hurting, but I did not come out the game.

It wasn't until two days later that I found out that I tore my lateral meniscus. I was hurt emotionally because my life dream was to play in the NFL. As a kid, I was raised to be a star athlete and play five to ten years in the NFL. I kept my head up and trusted in God that He would make a way for me. After I was placed on injured reserve, I was released after the third game week. I was blessed to get an accredited season, and in December of 2009, the Detroit Lions picked me up onto their practice squad. I signed a future contract after the season and was later cut after the 2010 NFL draft. Having just one game of film hurt my chances because coaches want to see consistency. I was at a new position with a small amount of film to evaluate me as a player.

In 2010, I decided to enter the United Football League and play for the Las Vegas Locos. I went to Arizona for a workout. In front of Jim Fassel, the former New York Giants coach, I ran a 4.14 in the forty-yard dash. Coach Fassel, in a newspaper article, said in all his years of coaching, I was the fastest player he has seen. I played a full season in the UFL as a kick returner and defensive back.

In 2011, I decided to run professional indoor track. I ran three indoor meets and qualified for the USA Indoor Championships. I placed fifth in the sixty meters, and my time was a 6.63.

CHAPTER 16

New Supplements

In 2012, when I was working to get back onto an NFL team, I was working at Sprouts Farmers Market as a vitamin clerk. I found a supplement on the shelf called deer antler velvet. At first, I was hesitant to take the product because it stated that IGF-1 was in the product, and I knew from studying the banned substance list that it was a banned substance. I always took pride in myself that I never cheated or took anything illegal during competition to help me become great. When I studied it out, I found out that the IGF-1 in the supplement was a natural form of IGF-1 and not the synthetic kind that they test for. I also found out that IGF-1 is naturally found in colostrum, which is breast milk. Colostrum is milk that comes from a mammal in the first seventy-two hours after they give birth. The growth factors, which are the makeup of HGH (human growth hormone), are given to the baby through the mother's milk to trigger the baby to grow. There are also immunoglobulins to help boost the baby's immune system. In order to see a benefit from taking colostrum, an athlete would need to take up to twenty grams a day for the IGF-1. I decided to try the deer antler out, and little did I know that this would become my favorite supplement. I took deer antler pills and tincture together, and I noticed an increase in my oxygen, endurance, strength, and recovery. To be honest, I felt like a mythical Greek god. My endurance and mental alertness increased, and I was able to do two to three tasks at one time. I remember training three to four times a day without feeling a tremendous amount of soreness.

I started giving my wife, Alesha, deer antler, and she became a totally different person. It was almost as if she went back to being eighteen years old again. She had more energy, increased libido, and an increased focus.

There have been some deer antler products that I have tried and did not work at all. In order to see benefits with deer antler, you have to take large amounts of it. In the pill form, I would take three to four pills when it was 10x extracted. There have been some products that are horrible and are only out there to make money. I can tell you this: the best deer antler tincture is made by Surthrival. They make a platinum bottle of elk antler, which is really strong. I have taken that product three times. Their elk antler is definitely one of my favorite supplements. It's a great product. Expensive, but worth it!

Taking deer antler tincture, I knew that I was going to have to deal with a lot of opinions that its use is not okay for the NFL. There was a media issue with Ray Lewis about him using the deer antler spray to recover faster from his triceps injury. I always made sure I did my research so I could respond with an intelligent answer if someone were to criticize me for using the supplement. I would state that the deer antler velvet is all-natural. It comes from the antlers of a deer in velvet stage. They cut the antlers off and clean it to get rid of any bacteria. After the cleaning is finished, they chop up the antler and separate them from top, middle, and bottom. The top part of the antler is the most potent part because in velvet stage the antlers are still growing. The majority of the growth factors are located in the top. Once they are packaged, the distributors can sell them in powder form, tincture, or pills. There is nothing synthetic put into the supplement. My other defense for this supplement is if the NCAA, NFL, WADA, and IOC decided to ban deer antler, then they would have to ban colostrum as well. It also contains growth factors IGF-1. How can you ban antlers from a deer and milk? It's hard to do something like that, and they know it. There is an article online that the WADA has lifted their ban of the use of deer antler for sport. They make it clear that if you do take it, you are taking it at your own risk. Always do the research for yourself and find out how the testing works to get a *full* understanding before you commit to taking a supplement.

Pine Pollen is another supplement that Surthrival makes, which is really potent and powerful. This plant is the male part of the pine, which pollinates the female to produce more pine trees. Pine Pollen contains natural plant hormones of DHEA and testosterone. These plant hormones are different from human hormones by 1-2 molecules. When taking pine pollen, you can get all of the benefits of DHEA and testosterone without the side effects of stopping your own production of testosterone. I was in the best shape of my life when I added the deer antler and Pine Pollen to my supplement regimen.

I got invited to the Detroit Lions Rookie Minicamp in 2013. I was taking my drug test, blood testing, and physicals. My resting heart rate was forty-four beats per minute. The doctor was a little concerned because it was low, but I was in tremendous amount of shape. Your heart does not have to work as hard when you have good cardiovascular exercise. My workouts at weight lifting became easier. I read a book called the *Westside Barbell*, which had information about the conjugate system. I tried it myself, and it worked great for me. I was able to get my bench press max to 405 lbs., and I weighed 180 lbs. This was a completely raw bench press, no shirt or straps.

The supplements and great programming took me to a higher level in training. The feeling I had was something I've never felt before. To be honest, I felt *powerful!* I could sometimes feel energy surges going through my body, but I had complete control over it. Many people turn to caffeine for energy, but it's hard to control. A big side effect of caffeine is jittery, nervousness, and there is a huge crash from it later in the day. The deer antler velvet and Pine Pollen, and my other supplements always gave me sustainable energy. I felt like I was eighteen years old even though I was twenty-six. I have to admit that while I was on these supplements, I felt invincible. A man can become very prideful if he is not aware on how to manage his thoughts. If you are a person who has very little self-control, I would suggest you stay away from these particular supplements.

CHAPTER 17

Green Superfood & Diet

The green superfood that I started to take in 2011 was ORAC-Energy Greens made by Paradise Herbs. This herbal supplement is great because its ORAC value, which stands for oxygen radical absorption capacity is forty thousand. This means that it helps the body get rid of and prevent free radicals, which can lead to or cause cancer. I use this supplement for overall health and well-being. Many people get cancer from having high hormones in their body, and they can't expel the hormones from the liver. The ORAC-Energy Greens help you get rid of and balance out your hormones. Another cause of cancer is too much inflammation in the body or an overload of cytokines, which triggers signaling molecules called prostaglandins to tell the body to inflame.

The ORAC-Energy Greens also contain wheat grass, barley, kale, spinach, broccoli, alfalfa, camu-camu, acerola berry, spirulina, chlorella, milk thistle, artichoke leaf, grape seed, ginger, maca root, turmeric, probiotics, and prebiotics. I would get a daily cleanse and detox from this supplement. These greens help expel harmful chemicals and toxins in the body. I have been taking this supplement for years and will continue to take this supplement until the day I die. If it's not ORAC-Energy Greens, it will be another superfood complex closest to it.

Diet

My diet has changed a lot since 2012. While on my new supplements, my hunger levels increased dramatically. I could eat a large Papa John's BBQ chicken pizza by myself. After I ate my pizza, I would take my greens and deer antler powder to help burn calories faster while I slept. I would wake up the next morning feeling light as a feather. My other favorite food is oatmeal. I did some studies on oatmeal and found that it had benefits of freeing up bound testosterone in the body. *Avena sativa* is the scientific name of oatmeal, and it binds to SHBG (sex hormone binding globulin) to help free up testosterone. When testosterone is free, it can then be used by the muscles. I always make sure that I, at least, eat oatmeal every morning and before a competition. I eat the organic oatmeal with less sugar because too much sugar defeats the purpose of oatmeal. Sugar has many harmful effects on the human body. One ingredient to stay away from is high fructose corn syrup. It has no nutritional value and is known as a toxin.

Whenever I'm searching for food, I always read the ingredient list. The ingredients I check for are high fructose corn syrup, soy, and other carcinogens that can harm your health. The soy that is in the market today is not the best choice because it is unfermented. If you are going to eat soy, please make sure it is fermented.

It is also good to eat food that has a short shelf-life. Food that has preservatives or was made with high heat has lost a lot of important nutrients. It can be difficult to find the right foods that are not highly processed. My advice to people looking to better their health is to start out with a green superfood supplement. Whenever I eat at a fast-food restaurant, I always consume my greens right after to counteract some of the bad ingredients in the food. If you put good nutrients into your body, then your body will function properly.

Chapter 18

Training Athletes

In 2011, I became a certified fitness trainer with ISSA. I trained Trent Totten who saw great results. I started working with Trent toward the end of his sophomore year. He was one of my favorite clients because he listened to everything I told him to do. On his initial assessment test, his barbell flat bench press max was at 145 lbs., and his forty-yard dash was a 5.8. I worked with him on certain programs, and he was supplementing with creatine, beta-alanine, protein, and L-arginine-ornithine. After three months of training, his bench press max increased to 225 lbs. and his forty-yard dash dropped to a 5.2. After a year and half of training with Trent, his bench press max was now at 315 lbs. and his forty-yard dash was a 4.98.

Another athlete who experienced multiple results through my training is Marcus Curry. He was a running back for Texas State and dealt with some previous injuries before training with me. His forty-yard dash time for his pro day was a 4.77 hand time, and he said he ran that slightly hurt. He also competed in the NFL Regional combine in 2013, and his time was a 4.68. We trained for about three months, and I slowly introduced him to my supplement regimen. I don't rush people to supplement with everything because it can be too much for most people. Marcus took every supplement except the deer antler and the pine pollen. I do not recommend those two supplements to athletes, but if they ask, I inform them to do their own research. We tested him in the forty-yard dash on a partial electronic laser timed system, and he ran a time of 4.52. This was great, considering his official time before which was a 4.77 in the NFL offices.

Rashod Favors, from the University of Oklahoma, had great test results at his NFL Pro Day in 2015. He was a linebacker and his weight when he started was at 266 lbs. We had to get him down to an ideal weight to run a faster time, and he was only six feet tall. After about two and a half months of training, he had his pro day and posted a time of 4.66 laser, fully automatic. His hand time was a 4.58, and his weight was 253 lbs. I watched his forty online, and he could have ran so much faster. He popped straight up and skipped a majority of his drive phase. I believe he could have ran a 4.4 hand time and a 4.5 laser. I was still proud of his work and results, which were amazing!

CHAPTER 19

Epilogue

I hope my book has helped you as an athlete, bodybuilder, or a health enthusiast looking to gain an edge in competition or life. A lot of people would look at my picture on the front cover and assume I was taking illegal synthetic steroids. I would always laugh to myself saying, "If they only knew." Well, now you know. I wanted to share my knowledge and experiences so people can see I am a natural athlete, known as the world's most jacked athlete.

A big part of my success was the time I spent studying training and supplement manuals since I was fourteen. I minored in exercise science in college, and a majority of my scientific background was self-taught. I appreciate the information I learned from Kevin Ensenat, ISSA, athlete builder, and Westside Barbell books. I am grateful to Sprouts Vitamin Department and VitaminShoppe for hiring me years ago to help expand my knowledge of supplements. I do not know everything, and I will never say I know everything when it comes to fitness. I am always open to learning, so I can continue to grow. Some people may not agree with my training or supplements, but one thing they can't deny are my results.

It is always good to check with your doctor to make sure you can take the supplements that I mentioned in the book. Every human being is different and has different genetic makeups. Please do not assume you will look like me or have the same speed by doing everything I wrote in this book. If you have any questions, feel free to reach out to me through my Facebook page or Instagram page.

God bless!